The FIRST BOOK of
SPACE TRAVEL

REVISED AND REWRITTEN

Library of Congress Catalog Card Number: 63-16910
Printed in the United States of America
by Polygraphic Company of America, Inc.

THE *FIRST BOOK* OF
SPACE TRAVEL

written and illustrated by
JEANNE BENDICK

768

FRANKLIN WATTS, INC.

575 LEXINGTON AVENUE • NEW YORK 22

WHAT SPACE IS

Do you ever stop to think that someday you may be traveling into space? You certainly may. If you are going to be an explorer or a weatherman, an astronomer or a builder, a doctor or a pilot, a teacher or a researcher, a mother or a farmer, space may be your place.

You may stay in space, or just travel through it. You may be there to look down at the earth or up at the stars. But will you know space when you get there?

Do you know where space is?

Do you know what is in it?

Do you know *what* space is?

Space is the immense emptiness through which move the sun and the other stars, the moons and the planets, the clouds of gas from which stars are born. There is no air in space. There is no heat. There is no sound. Some people think that space goes on forever, without end. The word for this endlessness is *infinity*.

7

HOW BIG IS SPACE?

The distances in space are so great that, no matter how hard you try, you can't *really* imagine them. In a very fast airplane, going two thousand miles an hour, it would take you five days to reach the moon, our nearest neighbor in space. In that fast airplane, going two thousand miles an hour, it would take you five years to reach the sun. If you traveled at the same speed toward Pluto, the most distant planet in our solar system, you would not get there for 225 years.

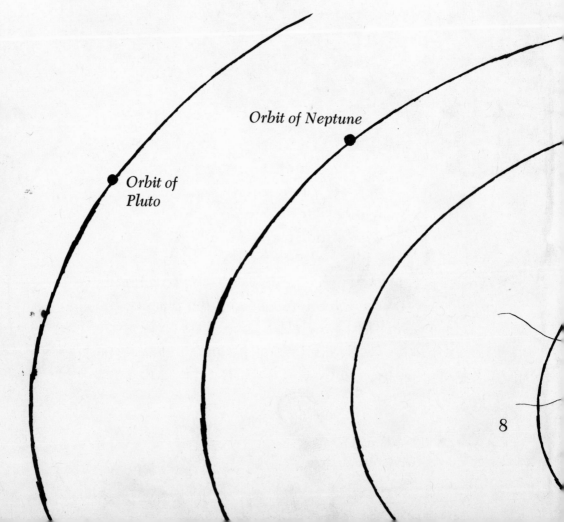

Orbit of Neptune

*Orbit of
Pluto*

Our solar system ("sol" means "sun") is made up of the star we call the sun and the nine planets that whirl around it in great paths called *orbits*. If you look at the picture you will see how close our planet, the earth, seems to the sun, although we are 93 million miles away. Some of the other planets are so far from the sun that very little of its heat reaches them. From these planets the sun looks merely like a bright star.

Our solar system is just a speck in the *universe*, which is all of space and all the stars and planets in it. Our solar system in the universe is no larger than a single grain of sand on all the beaches of the world.

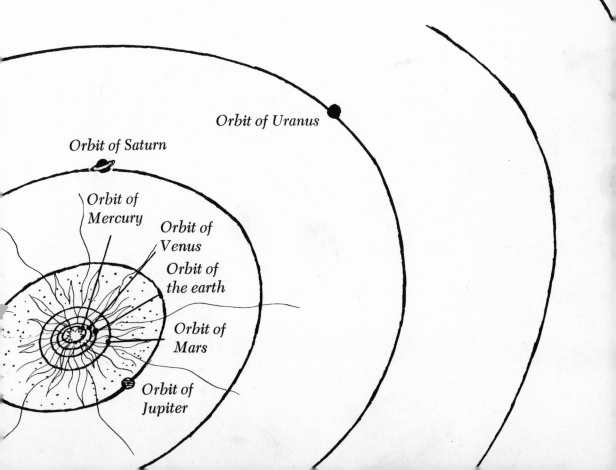

*The Milky Way is
made of billions
of stars*

Our sun is here

Our sun is part of a star family or *galaxy* called the Milky Way. In the Milky Way there are about a hundred billion stars, many of them brighter than our sun. The nearest of these stars is 26 trillion miles away. No matter how hard you try, you can't really imagine the size of our own galaxy. A rocket going 3,600 miles an hour would take two billion years to cross it. Yet out across space are millions of billions of galaxies.

Space is so big that measuring its distances in miles is inconvenient. Instead of miles we measure in *light-years*. Light is the fastest thing we know; it travels about 186,000 miles a second. A light-year is the distance light travels in one year; that is, about 6,000,000 million miles. You would have to travel back and forth across North America almost two billion times before you could travel the distance of one light-year. Yet some distances in space are measured in *billions* of light-years.

Space between the stars is called *interstellar* space. Space within our solar system is called *interplanetary* space. All of our travels in space will be interplanetary. Even if someday we find a way to travel as fast as light itself, it does not seem as if there will be time enough in a lifetime to travel among the stars.

WHAT IS IN SPACE?

A comet

There will be lots to see in the interplanetary space of our own solar system. Besides the planets and their moons there are thousands of asteroids — lumps of rock, some as big as small moons, others smaller than big mountains. Most of them travel between the orbits of Mars and Jupiter.

There are comets — immense clusters of frozen gases and dust — which travel in regular orbits, too. When comets come near the sun they usually develop tails of gas, millions of miles long.

There are billions of meteors — some as large as houses, but most as small as grains of sand. When meteors strike our atmosphere, they burn. We call them "shooting stars."

Does this sound as if space were crowded? A single dust mote in an empty barn is more crowded than the things in space.

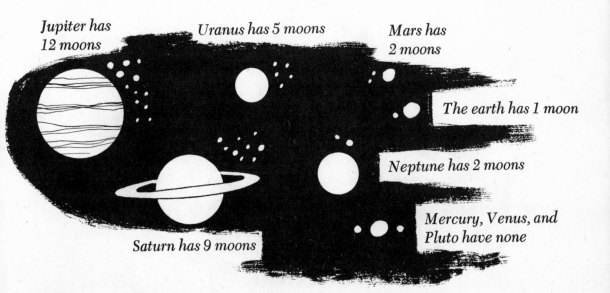

Jupiter has 12 moons

Uranus has 5 moons

Mars has 2 moons

The earth has 1 moon

Neptune has 2 moons

Mercury, Venus, and Pluto have none

Saturn has 9 moons

WHERE SPACE BEGINS

When you look up at the sky in the daytime, you can usually see the sun, sometimes the moon, and once in a while you can see other planets, if you know just where to look. But you can't see out into the far reaches of space. Billions and billions of air particles reflect the sun, and you can't see past them.

Our planet, earth, is wrapped in a quilt of air called the *atmosphere*, which is made of billions of tiny bits of different gases. Most of the atmosphere is a gas called *nitrogen*. About one particle in five is a gas called *oxygen*. The people and animals on the earth need oxygen to breathe.

As the earth travels through space,
>turning like a top,
>circling the sun,
>moving through our galaxy with the rest of the solar system,
>and through the universe with our galaxy,

Our galaxy, the Milky Way, moves through the universe

Our solar system moves through the galaxy

The earth rotates around the sun,

and spins like a top

it carries its atmosphere along. This is very fortunate, because we could not live an instant without atmosphere. We need oxygen to breathe. We need the weight of the atmosphere pushing on our bodies, else we would explode. We need the atmosphere to shield us from meteors and from the sun, which could otherwise destroy every living thing with its ultraviolet rays.

The atmosphere is hundreds of miles thick, but it is not the same from top to bottom. At the bottom, the air particles are very close together. Here is the air we live in. It is called the *troposphere*.

Two or three miles up there are still plenty of air particles, but not enough for people to breathe. Even on the highest mountains the air is very thin. Airplanes flying over three miles high must carry extra air inside.

Air is always pushing on you from all sides

13

The *stratosphere* begins about eight miles up. There are still many air particles in the stratosphere. In its upper part is a layer of a particular kind of oxygen called ozone, which screens out many of the sun's ultraviolet rays.

About 50 miles up, there are not enough air particles to make the light we call daylight. The sky is a very dark blue, and a little higher it is completely black, even in daytime. Here is the *ionosphere*, which is about 200 miles deep. Its particles are electrically charged by the X rays and ultraviolet rays from the sun. This electrified layer reflects the radio waves we broadcast around the earth.

Above the ionosphere, about 250 miles up, starts the exosphere. This is the last layer of the atmosphere, reaching up 700 or 800 miles above the earth. It has almost no air particles at all. The exosphere contains some charged particles which are part of the earth's *magnetic field.* (You probably know that the earth is a giant magnet, with magnetic force around it just like that in any other magnet.)

The Van Allen radiation belts begin in the exosphere, too. These are belts of electrons, trapped by the earth's magnetic field, that extend thousands of miles out into space.

Where does space begin? You might say 50 miles up, where the sky is always black. You might say in the exosphere, where there are only a few puffs of air in thousands of miles. You might say space begins above the exosphere where there is nothing except, here and there, one hydrogen atom billions of times smaller than the smallest grain of sand.

People can breathe comfortably only here

14

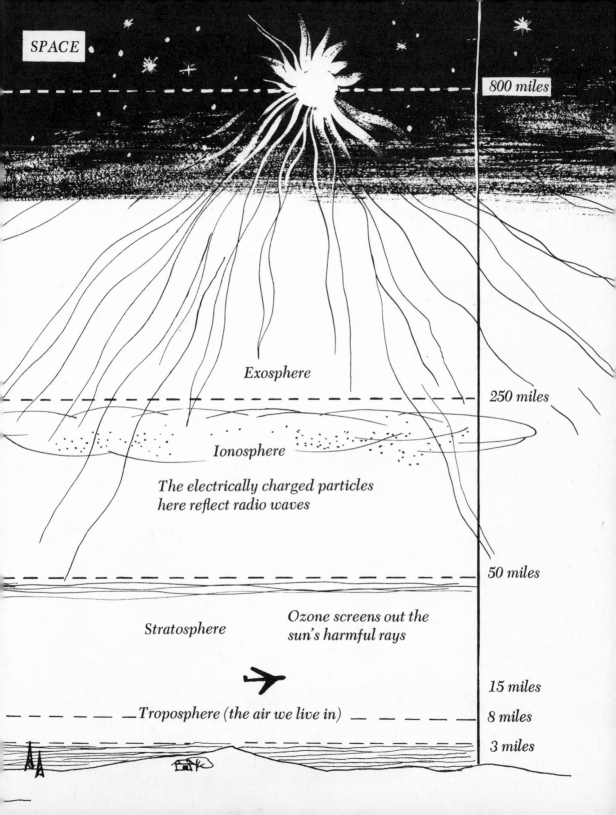

SPACE

800 miles

Exosphere

250 miles

Ionosphere

The electrically charged particles
here reflect radio waves

50 miles

Stratosphere

Ozone screens out the
sun's harmful rays

15 miles

Troposphere (the air we live in)

8 miles

3 miles

DREAMS OF SPACE
OR
IS ANYTHING WRONG WITH THESE STORIES?

Long before we used airplanes or automobiles or even electricity, space travel started off in the minds of storytellers. Some of the stories we call science fiction have been stepping-stones into space.

The sun would heat the gas in here,

and the heated gas, escaping from the top, would fill the sail and make the ship rise

In 1656 some stories by Cyrano de Bergerac were published, imagining voyages to the moon and sun. He imagined a space ship that would be pulled up to the sun by hot gas escaping from its top. The gas was heated by the sun's rays shining on the ship. How does this idea sound to you? (See page 25.)

The space ship was fired at the moon at 25,000 miles an hour

Jules Verne was probably the most famous science fiction writer who ever lived. He imagined submarines, helicopters, and space rockets long before they were invented. In 1865, when he wrote *From The Earth To The Moon,* he sent his space travelers off in a shell fired out of a cannon. Do you think he had a good idea or not? (See page 21.)

In 1901 H. G. Wells wrote a story called *The First Men in the Moon.* Mr. Wells imagined a gravity screen. It opened and shut like a Venetian blind, cutting the ship off from gravity or letting gravity through. Do you think we can cut gravity off? (For the answer to this one, turn the page.)

You might enjoy reading these oldest science fiction stories. You might enjoy writing some of your own.

THE PROBLEM OF GETTING UP

1. BEATING GRAVITY

The earth holds us close. No magnet ever held a nail tighter than the earth holds us. No spider web ever held a bug better, no trap ever held an animal more securely. You are almost glued to the earth, and so is everything else on it.

How high can you jump? Not very high, because the earth pulls you back. If you drop a rock or a ball, a fork or a feather, they fall to earth. The earth holds everything tight: soil and mountains, buildings and birds, people and the atmosphere. It even keeps the moon from flying farther out into space. The earth's pull on everything on its surface or close to it is called *gravity*. The farther away from the earth you get, the weaker the pull of gravity becomes.

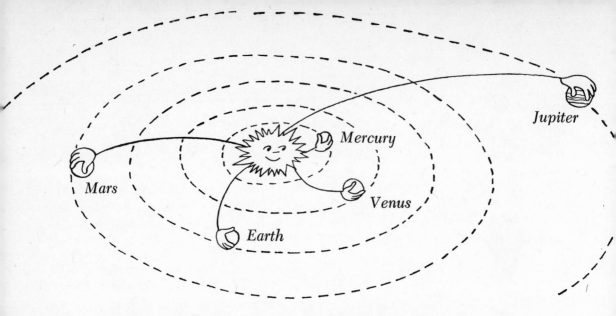

Mercury

Mars

Venus

Earth

Jupiter

The sun has gravity, too, much stronger than the earth's because the sun is much larger and heavier. The sun's gravity holds the solar system together. The moon has gravity, too, but less than the earth does, because the moon is smaller. All the other planets and stars have gravity. But it is the earth's gravity that earthmen have to beat before they can get out into space.

Nobody has ever found a way to shut gravity off. So far, we know of only one way to beat it, and that is with speed. We have to get away from the earth fast enough to escape into space before the earth's gravity can pull us back. The speed that is needed to escape the earth's gravity has its own name: *escape velocity*. (Velocity is another word for speed.)

We are used to traveling very fast on earth — hundreds of miles an hour in jet passenger planes, thousands in experimental planes. The earth's escape velocity is much, much faster. It is more than 25,000 miles an hour.

2. GETTING THROUGH THE ATMOSPHERE

If you fire a shell out of a cannon, it goes very, very fast. You know that it doesn't go as fast as the escape velocity, however, because even if you point the cannon straight up, the shell always falls back to earth. Could you build a cannon powerful enough to fire a shell — or a space ship — out into space? Maybe you could, but it would never get there. It would burn up before it got through the lowest layer of the earth's atmosphere.

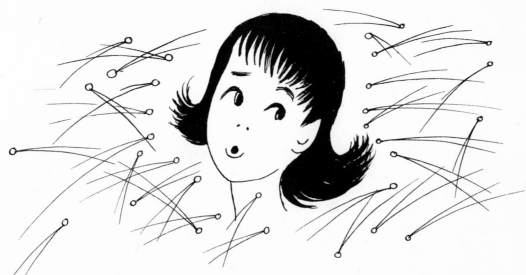

Down where the atmosphere is thick, billions and billions of particles or *molecules* of air zip about in every direction, as fast as bullets. They don't hurt you because they are very small, only about one hundred-millionth of an inch across. Compared to them, you move very slowly.

The faster anything moves, the more air particles bump and jiggle and rub against it, and the hotter it gets. The bumping and rubbing of molecules is called *friction*. Friction makes heat. When you go down a slide fast, you feel friction on the seat of your pants. By rubbing two sticks together, you can start a fire with friction. Meteorites coming into the earth's atmosphere burn up because of friction. Friction is one of the problems of fast flight. The interiors of very fast jets have to be refrigerated so that the pilots won't frizzle.

You can see that if you started a space machine off toward space *too* fast it would burn up. It must start slowly, gathering enough speed to reach escape velocity after it has passed through the thickest part of the atmosphere.

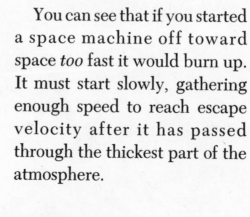

If the space machine goes too fast, the friction of the atmosphere will burn it up

It has to start slowly, then gather speed

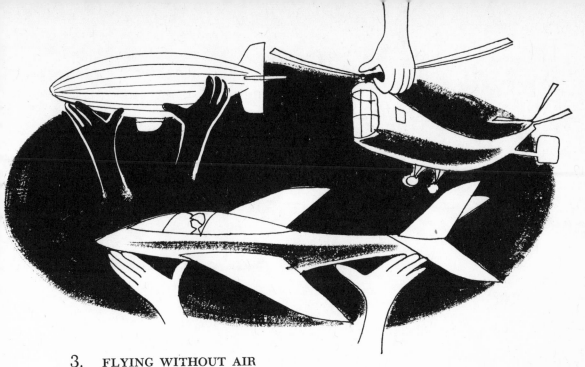

3.   FLYING WITHOUT AIR

Once you are through the atmosphere, you have another problem. What will hold you up? Air helps hold up airships and airplanes and helicopters. Air keeps their engines running, too, because fuel cannot burn without oxygen. Even jet planes scoop air into their engines to keep their fuel burning. But there is no air in space.

Air scoop

ROCKETS

What will you ride into space?

You will need a machine that will start slowly, then build up a speed of more than 25,000 miles an hour. You will need a machine that can fly right through the earth's atmosphere out into airless space and keep on going.

You will need a rocket.

HOW A ROCKET WORKS

A rocket can be one of the simplest engines in the world. If you take a tube nearly full of solid fuel, with the front end closed and the back end open, and set fire to the fuel, you have a rocket.

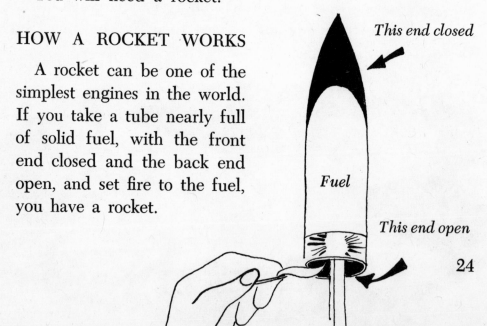

This end closed

Fuel

This end open

All rockets, even very complicated ones, work in just about the same way.

The burning fuel turns into hot gases that push hard, from inside, against the closed front and sides of the rocket. But the gases can't go out through the front and sides. They are thrown back, out through the hole in the rear; and as they go out, they push the rocket ahead. The push of hot gases against the rocket walls is called *thrust*.

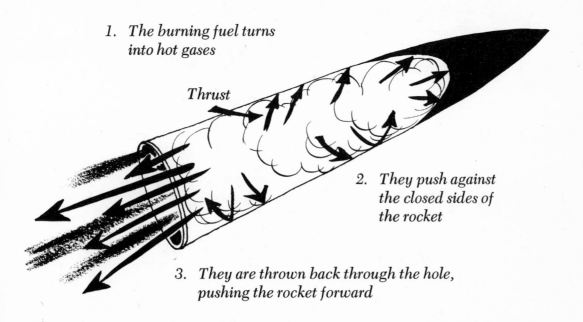

1. *The burning fuel turns into hot gases*

Thrust

2. *They push against the closed sides of the rocket*

3. *They are thrown back through the hole, pushing the rocket forward*

Thrust is the measurement of a rocket's power. It is figured in pounds. New rocket engines have a thrust of millions of pounds.

WHY A ROCKET WORKS

Isaac Newton, the scientist who stated the law of gravity, also figured out what he called the "laws of motion."

The *first law of motion* says, in part, that anything that is not moving will stay motionless unless something pushes or pulls it. Once it is started, it will keep moving until some force acts to stop it.

Something has to start things moving

Then something has to stop them. (Even the push or resistance of air against something will stop it.)

The *second law of motion* tells us that the harder you push something, the faster it will go in the direction you push it.

The harder you push, the faster it will go

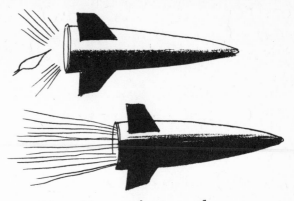

These first two laws of motion are important in starting a rocket off. Something has to be done to set it in motion, then the more push or thrust it has, the faster it will go.

Although there were no rockets in Isaac Newton's time, the *third law of motion* explains what makes a rocket work. It says that every action has an equal reaction in the opposite direction.

Another way of saying this is as follows:

When something is pushed forward, there is a backward push of the same amount. When something moves forward, something else moves backward the same amount.

Did you ever see a picture of a cannon being fired? When the shell shoots forward, the cannon jumps backward.

When a boat goes forward in the water, the water goes back behind it.

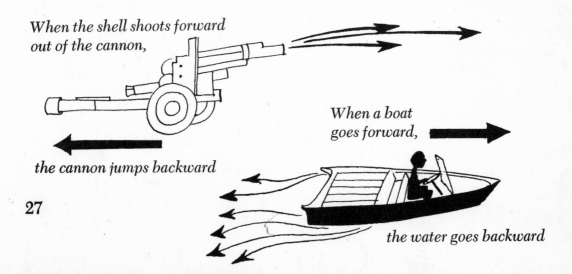

When the shell shoots forward out of the cannon,

the cannon jumps backward

When a boat goes forward,

the water goes backward

When a bat hits a baseball, the ball goes one way, and the bat slows down. Sometimes you can't see the second motion, but it is always there.

When a jet of hot gas shoots backward out of a jet airplane's exhaust, the airplane goes forward. When a jet of burning gas shoots backward out of a rocket, the rocket goes forward.

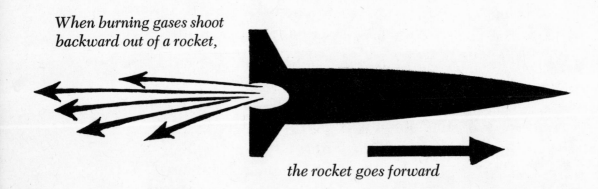

When burning gases shoot backward out of a rocket,

the rocket goes forward

But a rocket goes much faster than an airplane. It goes so fast that it doesn't need air to support it. Air only gets in the way and slows it down.

A fast jet plane and a rocket look much alike. They are both slim and streamlined. They have small, swept-back wings. A jet of hot gases pushes them ahead. The jet plane needs oxy-

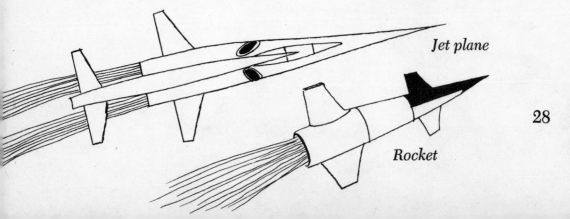

Jet plane

Rocket

gen from the atmosphere to make its fuel burn; nothing can burn without oxygen. A rocket does not depend on oxygen from outside, however. Inside itself it carries everything it needs to propel it (or make it go): fuel and the *oxidizer* to keep the fuel burning.

FUEL FOR A ROCKET

Rockets can use either solid or liquid fuels.

A rocket that uses solid fuel is called a solid-propellant rocket. It can be quite simple. The fuel and the oxidizer, mixed together in a solid lump, are in the burning chamber. As the solid fuel burns, hot gas is thrown out of the rear of the rocket.

A solid-fuel rocket works like this

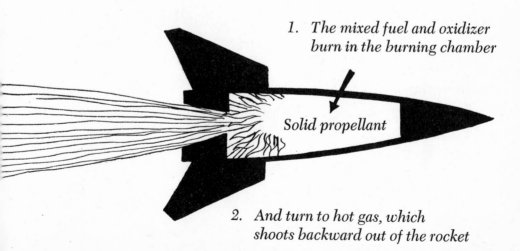

1. *The mixed fuel and oxidizer burn in the burning chamber*

Solid propellant

2. *And turn to hot gas, which shoots backward out of the rocket*

A liquid-propellant rocket works like this

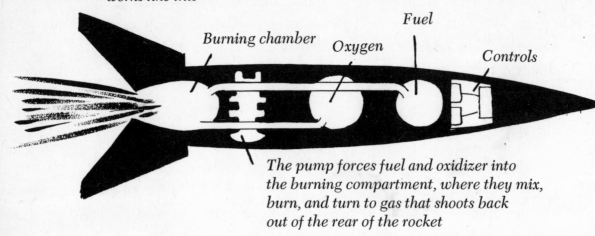

Burning chamber

Oxygen

Fuel

Controls

The pump forces fuel and oxidizer into the burning compartment, where they mix, burn, and turn to gas that shoots back out of the rear of the rocket

A liquid-propellant rocket is more complicated. The oxygen and the fuel are stored separately, in liquid form, and must be pumped into the burning chamber to mix, burn, and form the hot gas. A liquid-propellant rocket needs two fuel compartments, and a turbine to pump the fuels into the burning chamber.

A liquid-propellant rocket

A solid-fuel rocket

Small, thin rockets are solid-propellant rockets. Middle-sized ones might be either. Very large rockets are usually liquid - propellant. Sometimes rockets of both kinds are hitched together.

This rocket has a liquid-fuel motor,

and a solid-fuel booster

ROCKETS IN STAGES

Rockets are often made up of separate parts called *stages*. Each stage is a rocket in itself. Two or three or even four rockets are hitched together for the following reason.

As a rocket's fuel burns away, the section that held the fuel becomes a dead weight. The empty part has no job to do, and it slows the rocket down. But a multi-stage rocket — one with more than one stage — can operate without carrying the dead weight.

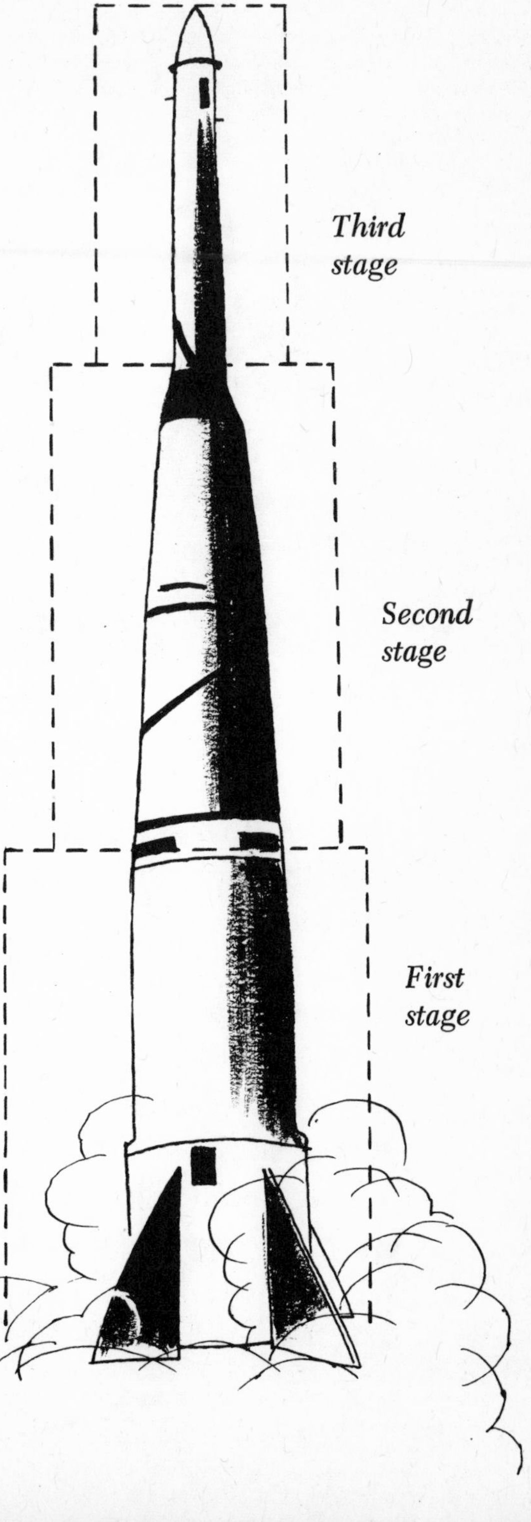

A three-stage rocket.
Each stage is different.

Third stage

Second stage

First stage

Third stage

Second stage

First the bottom stage is fired. When all of its fuel is burned, that stage drops away and the next stage fires. When its fuel is used up, that stage drops away too. Thus the rocket never carries any useless weight. Different kinds of rockets are often used as different stages, each designed to do a special job toward putting the *payload* where it is supposed to be.

First stage

32

THE PAYLOAD

The payload is what the rocket carries; it is the reason for sending the rocket up. In a Fourth of July skyrocket, the payload is a shower of stars. In a missile, the payload is a charge of explosive. In an exploring or *sounding* rocket, the payload is instruments for checking, observing, measuring, photographing, and reporting. The payload may be an earth satellite or a space probe. The payload may also be animals for scientific study, or men on their way into space.

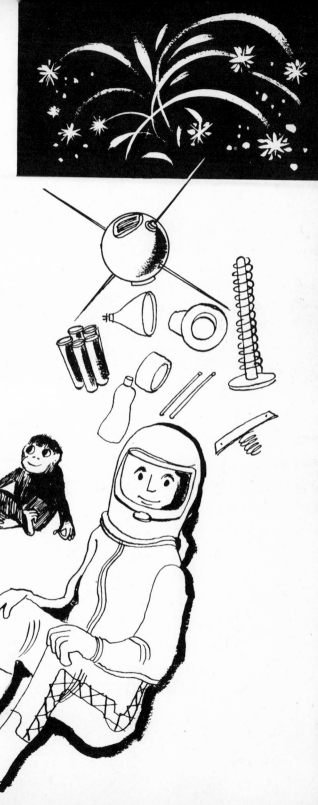

ABOUT MISSILES

Missiles are weapons.

If you throw a stone at someone, the stone is a missile. So is an arrow or a bullet or a bomb. A rocket built to be a missile has only one job: to destroy. Its payload is a charge of explosive and the fuse to set it off.

A *guided* missile is one that is guided or directed over most of its flight. If the missile is only aimed when it is launched, it is *unguided*.

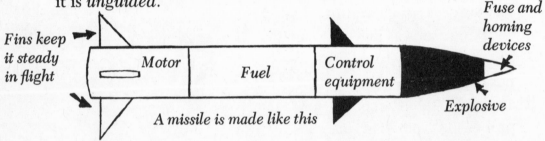

Fins keep it steady in flight

Motor   Fuel   Control equipment

Fuse and homing devices

Explosive

A missile is made like this

A *surface-to-surface* missile is launched from the ground or the sea, and directed at a target on the earth's surface, though it may be halfway round the world.

A *surface-to-air* missile is fired from the earth's surface (land or sea) at a target in the air.

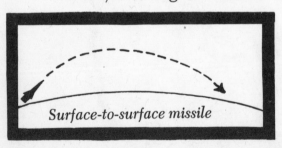

Surface-to-surface missile

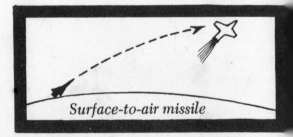

Surface-to-air missile

34

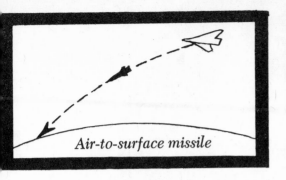

Air-to-surface missile

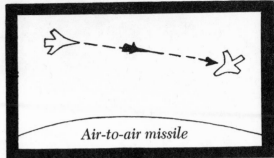

Air-to-air missile

An *air-to-surface* missile is fired from an aircraft at a target on the ground.

An *air-to-air* missile is launched in the air and directed at a target in the air.

Someday the same kinds of rockets that are now missiles will carry other payloads.

Surface-to-air rockets now launch satellites, manned capsules, and space probes. Someday they will carry supplies and people from earth to space stations, and air-to-surface rockets will carry things back.

Air-to-air rockets will carry supplies from planes to satellites, or from one satellite to another.

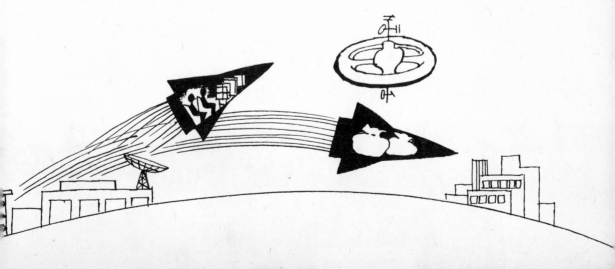

This is the telescope

The giant telescope at Mount Palomar in California

The mounting holds the telescope in position

The exploration of space began long before anyone ever imagined going there. It began when man first looked up at the stars. You can see the sun and the moon, most of the planets, and about six thousand stars with your eyes alone.

But if you want to see millions of stars, you need a telescope. Through the largest telescopes you can see *billions* of stars. The 200-inch telescope at Mount Palomar, in California, explores two billion light-years into space, farther than man himself could ever go.

Astronomers usually do their space exploring with a combination of telescope and camera. This team can follow, for hours, the pinpoint light of a star billions of miles away, photographing it through the eye of its clock-driven telescope.

Star clusters

The radio telescope at Jodrell Bank, in England

A radio telescope "hears" stars that are invisible to us. Many of these stars radiate powerful energy waves which astronomers can "tune in." A radio telescope is really a large aerial, set in the center of an immense reflector. Ten thousand people could sit in the reflector of the giant radio telescope at Jodrell Bank, in England.

Spectroscopes have told us many things about stars and planets. Every chemical element in the universe sends out its own pattern of colors and lines. A spectroscope is a kind of prism that separates these so that we can see what stars are made of, and what gases make up the atmospheres of our sister planets. Spectroscopes that work with cameras are called *spectrographs.*

Nebulae are immense clouds of dust and gases that form new stars

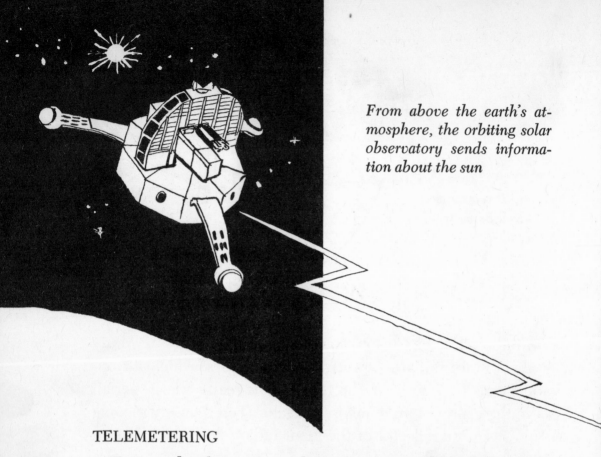

From above the earth's atmosphere, the orbiting solar observatory sends information about the sun

TELEMETERING

Eyes and telescopes, radio telescopes and spectroscopes explore space from the bottom of the atmosphere, where we live. There are many other ways of exploring space from earth. Most of them depend on the science of *telemetering*, or "measuring at a distance." In telemetering, information is sent to a distant observation station where it is recorded.

A rocket or a satellite is packed with instruments, each with a particular job to do. One might measure wind speeds, another might measure radiation, another heat; one might send pictures. A hundred instruments could be gathering a hundred different kinds of information. All the instruments are connected into a tiny radio transmitter, which relays their observations back to earth.

At a telemetering station on the ground, the information is received and separated. Information from each instrument is sent to its own receiving set in the telemetering station, where the signal is changed into one that can be read, and recorded.

The information is constant; by means of it, scientists in a control center can keep a continual watch on an astronaut's pulse, for example, or can tell, from second to second, how hot a rocket's shell is.

Satellites sometimes store the readings from their instruments on a kind of tape recorder. When the satellite passes over its ground station it receives a special signal that starts the tape recorder transmitting its information.

EXPLORING WITH SATELLITES AND ROCKETS

Scientists send their eyes and ears out into space in satellites and rockets.

Sounding rockets are the advance explorers. *Sounding* means "exploring." A sailor sounds the ocean depths with his lead line, and a meteorologist sounds the lower atmosphere with a weather balloon. There are many kinds of sounding rockets for carrying different payloads and exploring at different heights.

Aerobee *is a sounding rocket*

This is as far as sounding rockets go

Radius of the earth

Generally the rockets work in the earth's atmosphere, above balloon height, which is 20 miles, and below the lowest satellite altitude, which is about 125 miles.

Sometimes sounding rockets are used farther up, but they never go higher than one radius of the earth — the distance from the center of the earth to its crust. They perform experiments where the payload must be recovered, because sounding rockets always return to earth. They do not go into orbit.

Sounding rockets flight-test new instruments. They study the atmosphere, which is the source of all our weather. They study magnetism and radiation and electrical particles.

Farther out, their instruments investigate sunspots, solar flares, and the effect of storms on the sun.

Rockets that go deeper into space, out through the earth's magnetic field and radiation belts, are called *geoprobes*.

The rockets that go farthest of all, as far as the moon, or out to the planets and beyond, are called *deep space probes*.

Only the sounding rockets return to earth. The others travel out into space, sending back their information across thousands and millions of miles.

The space probes that go to the moon or out among the planets, send back information throughout their journeys. Many of these spacecraft have such delicate control systems that they can be commanded from earth, even when they are far out in space. *Command* is the opposite of telemetering. A ground transmitter sends a signal to the spacecraft, to correct a course, turn power off and on, start cameras or other equipment, or even soften a landing.

MARINER *is a deep space probe*

PROSPECTOR is designed to move across the surface of the moon

Spacecraft that are planned for unmanned landings on the moon or the planets carry instruments to analyze minerals or chemicals that they may find, to take television pictures, and to see if there is any kind of life.

Sticky strings, reaching out onto the surface, draw samples back into the spacecraft to be analyzed. Then the results can be telemetered back to earth.

Some spacecraft are designed to travel slowly across the surface they are exploring.

Sometimes a spacecraft is designed to be used both as a probe and a satellite. The probe might land, while its satellite twin would orbit, sending back different kinds of information.

SURVEYOR can carry 300 pounds of instruments

It can land or orbit

SATELLITES

The moon, revolving around the earth, is our natural satellite, but we have many kinds of man-made satellites, too. The best time for seeing satellites, if you know exactly where and when to look, is at sunset or dawn. They look like extra-bright, fast-moving stars.

Most satellites have no rocket power of their own. Even if a satellite is the last stage of a rocket, its power has burned out. After a satellite has been put into orbit (we'll talk about orbits on pages 48-49) it stays in its path, actually falling around the earth. It doesn't need any fuel to keep it going, and it goes very fast — faster than a bullet. A bullet goes about 4,000 miles an hour; a satellite goes 18,000 miles an hour or more.

The closer to earth a satellite is, the smaller its orbit will be, and the more rapidly it will circle. But the closer to earth it is, the sooner it will come down as air friction slows it down.

The first earth satellite, Sputnik I, was 500 miles above the earth, and stayed up about two months. Vanguard I, about 2,000 miles up, could stay in orbit for hundreds of years.

If a satellite is close to earth, it takes less time to circle

A satellite with a larger orbit takes longer

Satellites tell us things about the earth, our atmosphere, and space. They are packed with equipment.

They carry instruments for measuring temperatures and changes in the atmosphere.

They count meteors and other particles.

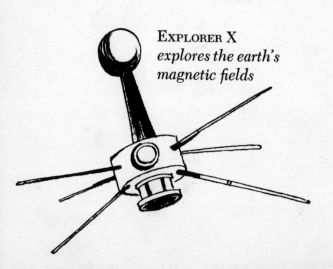

EXPLORER X *explores the earth's magnetic fields*

TELSTAR *is a television and telephone relay*

They measure cosmic rays, which are powerful radiations sent out by the sun and stars.

They chart the earth's magnetic fields and the belts of radiation. (More about these on pages 50-51.)

They report the weather as it forms around the earth.

They are relay stations for telephone and television.

They are navigation aids, like beacons in the sky.

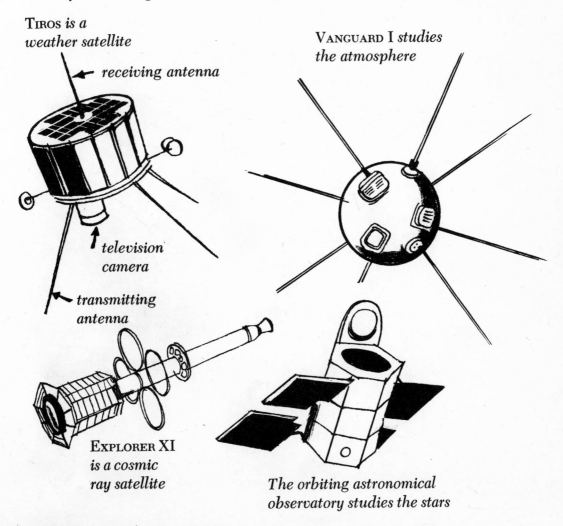

TIROS *is a weather satellite*

receiving antenna

VANGUARD I *studies the atmosphere*

television camera

transmitting antenna

EXPLORER XI *is a cosmic ray satellite*

The orbiting astronomical observatory studies the stars

Satellites orbiting the other planets, or the moon, send back information about them.

Big satellites will be space stations; people will live on them and work on them. They will be stopping places on the way to other satellites farther out in space, or on the way to other planets. They will have workshops and repair shops for building and fixing space ships. They will be supply depots.

If you have a good memory, you can tell your children and grandchildren that you remember when there was only the moon as a satellite.

LAUNCH VEHICLES

Satellites, sounding rockets, and probes are payloads. They are fired into space by other rockets called *launch vehicles.*

A launch vehicle is the first stage of a rocket, designed to launch a special payload into space. The heavier the payload, the bigger, more powerful, and more complicated the launch vehicle has to be, and the more thrust it must have.

A light launch vehicle, like SCOUT, can launch 150 pounds into space.

ATLAS is a medium launch vehicle. It can launch the MERCURY capsule, with an astronaut in it, into space.

When you see two names together, like ATLAS AGENA, it means that these two rockets together are used as a vehicle to launch the payload.

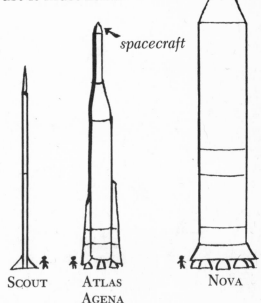

spacecraft

spacecraft

SCOUT   ATLAS   NOVA
        AGENA

ATLAS is the first stage and AGENA is the second. ATLAS AGENA is a medium launch vehicle too, but more powerful than ATLAS alone. It can launch 5,000 pounds.

NOVA is a heavy launch vehicle. It can launch a 150,000-pound payload to escape velocity. NOVA will launch the Apollo spacecraft, with three men aboard, to the moon.

47

ABOUT ORBITS

An orbit is a path, or a track. It is a route taken by a celestial body — that is, anything you see in the sky such as a sun or moon, a planet or satellite — when it circles another celestial body. The earth moves in an orbit around the sun. The moon moves in an orbit around the earth.

An orbit is almost never round. It is an ellipse, like this.

An orbit is not a circle, but an ellipse

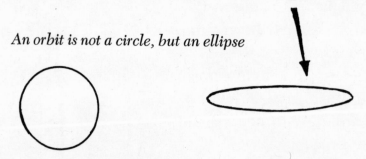

The orbits of the larger heavenly bodies do not change; the planets, moons, and comets have traveled the same paths for millions of years. Because of these unchanging orbits, our years are always the same length; we know when the moon will be new or full; and we can predict, hundreds of years in advance, when many of the comets will come and go.

We cannot control the orbit of our earth, but when we send satellites into the sky we can choose orbits for them. If we calculate carefully and aim the rocket that carries the satellite carefully, and shoot it at precisely the right instant, we can put a satellite into the orbit we have chosen.

But if any part of our careful planning goes wrong, the orbit will not be the one we intended. The satellite may go off into space, or come down sooner and faster than we had planned, or it may never come down at all. This would be mighty unpleasant if the satellite were carrying people.

Here are the words that give you information about an orbit, or, in other words, they give you *orbital data.*

The *period* is the length of time needed to complete an orbit. The period of the moon is 28 days. The period of Explorer I was 115 minutes.

The *inclination to the equator* is the angle at which the orbit of the satellite is tilted to the equator of the earth. It is measured in degrees, like any angle. The picture will show you what the inclination is.

The *perigee* is the point at which the orbit comes closest to earth.

The *apogee* is the point at which the orbit is farthest from earth. Perigee and apogee heights are measured in miles from the earth's surface.

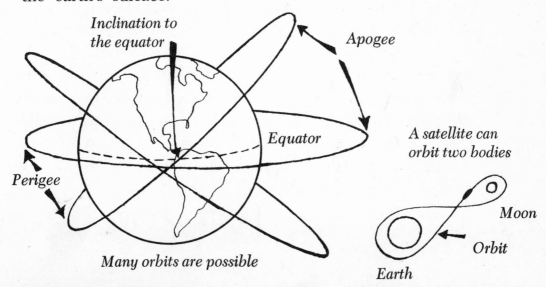

Inclination to the equator

Apogee

Equator

Perigee

A satellite can orbit two bodies

Moon

Orbit

Many orbits are possible

Earth

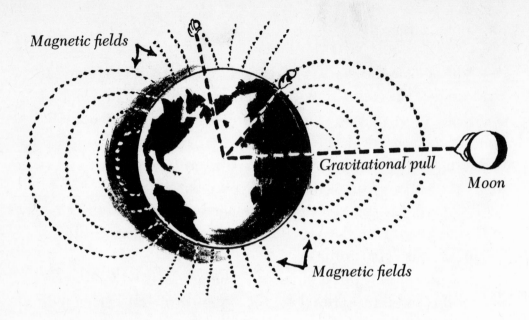

Magnetic fields

Gravitational pull

Moon

Magnetic fields

THE FIELDS IN SPACE

The "fields in space," which we sometimes talk about, are not like daisy fields or cornfields. A field in space is a region in space throughout which certain forces operate.

There are *gravitational* fields in space, and *magnetic* fields, and *electric* fields.

Gravitational fields are the regions around any heavenly body where that body's gravitational pull is operating. The gravitational pull of the sun is enormous, reaching out across millions and millions of miles to hold the planets in their orbits.

The earth's gravitational field is much smaller because the earth is much smaller, but it is very strong — strong enough to keep our feet anchored to earth, strong enough to keep our atmosphere in place, strong enough to hold the moon in its orbit.

50

The earth's gravitational field keeps man-made satellites in their orbits, too.

The earth's magnetic field is the region around the earth where magnetic forces operate. The earth is a giant magnet with a north and south pole like an ordinary bar magnet, so its magnetic field has the same sort of pattern.

Satellites have located a ring of electric current around the earth, sometimes two or three times as far as the earth's radius, sometimes ten times as far.

The Van Allen radiation belts are made of electrons and other *electromagnetic* particles trapped in the earth's magnetic field. (Nobody has ever been able to separate electricity from magnetism.) These particles seem to come directly from the sun, and nobody knows yet how dangerous their radiation might be to men traveling out into space.

The Van Allen belts are shaped like lopsided doughnuts

A SPACE SHIP FOR A MAN

When you are building a space ship to carry not only instruments as a payload, but people too, you have to think of many things.

The ship must be strong enough to stand the shock of take-off, the great changes in pressure, the heat of coming back into the earth's atmosphere, and the shock of landing.

It has to be light enough so that the launch vehicle can lift it into space.

It has to be able to stand tremendous changes in temperature, so that it will not crack in cold, or melt, or cook its passengers when it is very hot.

What would you build your ship of? Maybe you would make it of thin, thin sheets of metal, or of an alloy — that is, a combination of metals. You could strengthen it with thin strings of metal like this, or like this.

Or maybe you would make a sandwich of two thin sheets of metal with a very lightweight filler.

You could make it stronger, with air pressure from inside, like a balloon.

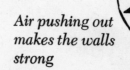

Air pushing out makes the walls strong

Maybe you could build your rocket out of ceramic, which is clay. Some ceramics are very strong and can stand tremendous heat. Furnaces for making steel are lined with ceramic brick, which stays hard at temperatures that melt steel.

A space ship for a man has to be like a little world. It has to contain its own atmosphere, like the one the man is used to on earth. He needs oxygen to breathe. Carbon dioxide, the waste gas human beings breathe out, has to be removed from the air. Man needs the right amount of air pressure on his body, or his blood would boil when he was about 12 miles up. He needs air conditioning so that he won't get too hot or too cold or too damp. All these things must be furnished him in the cabin of his spacecraft, and for extra protection, right in his space suit too.

The space ship needs two sets of controls: one for the space-man, and one that can be commanded from a control center on earth.

WOULD *YOU* MAKE A SPACEMAN?

Scientists who work with space flight divide the problems into two parts.

One has to do with designing good space machines.

The other has to do with the problems of man in space.

Space is not the natural place for earth creatures. We can live there only if we make it as much as possible like the kind of world we are used to. Even getting up into space is full of problems for a spaceman. How good would you be at the job?

First, there is the tremendous blast and pressure as the rocket takes off, fighting its way up, at great speed, against the force of gravity.

Then, if you are by yourself, there will be the terrible loneliness of being in space, cut off from every other human being.

NO GRAVITY

The strangest feeling of all is that of no **gravity** — of weight-lessness. On earth, gravity is pulling on us all **the** time. The more something weighs, the harder gravity pulls.

But when a spacecraft is in space, falling freely around the earth at a terrific speed, nothing has any weight at all. Every-thing is falling at the same speed. If everything in the space-craft were not bolted down, objects would be floating. If a spaceman were not fastened to his couch, he would be floating, too. He might float sideways, or with his feet higher than his head. There is no up or down. With weightlessness, most peo-ple feel wonderful, but a few feel a little sick and confused.

There is no up or down in space

TOO MUCH GRAVITY

Space experts use the word *acceleration* for a change of speed — either speeding up or slowing down. Both speeding up and slowing down change our feeling of weight.

The unit for measurement of gravity is called a g. As you walk about the earth, you have one g of gravity pulling on you.

If you are in an accelerating rocket, this force increases. Suppose you weigh 100 pounds. When the force increases to 2 g, you weigh 200 pounds. When it increases to 5 g, you weigh 500. At that point your head is too heavy to lift, or even turn. You can barely move a finger. The blood is pulled away from your head to your feet. But a powerful rocket, accelerating, might put a pull of 7 g on you. Could you bear it?

Yes, you could. Lying on a padded couch to fit your body, you could stand as much as 25 g.

Would you enjoy zero gravity?

Could you bear weighing five or six hundred pounds for a few minutes?

If you were turned end over end — and around, too — would you still know which way you were going?

Do you feel "gone" and miserable when you are very hot? Do you want to give up and lie down and not move at all when you are very cold?

Does a tremendous amount of noise confuse you so that you don't know what you're doing?

Do you hate to be in the house by yourself, or out of touch with other people?

Can you keep a thousand details in your mind, and still think quickly in an emergency?

How do you think you'd rate as a spaceman? Spacemen who pass all their tests are *tigers*. If you're a tiger, space is your place!

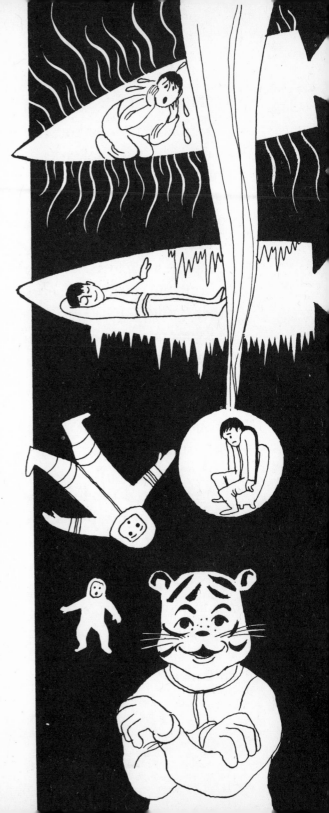

OUT INTO SPACE

You have trained and studied for years to get ready for your space trip. It has taken even longer to design and build a ship that will be capable of taking you into space and bringing you back safely.

Before you, other men have gone into space, first for a few hours, then for longer times.

Mathematicians have worked for months with computers, figuring out orbits and courses and times and speeds and many other things.

Every one of the thousands and thousands of parts in every stage of the launch vehicle and in your spacecraft has been checked and tested. If the smallest part isn't working properly, nothing starts.

Equipment and supplies have been assembled and checked. Once the rocket takes off, it will be too late to pick up anything you've forgotten. You can't run down to the corner store. Everything you need has to be inside the space ship, placed so that you can get at it safely and easily.

The control center is ready to send the rocket up, and to command the equipment in the craft whenever it is necessary. The telemetric instruments are already at work. The computers are at work. The control center is in touch with tracking stations all over the world. They will provide constant information about your craft's location in space, its orbit, and its guidance.

On the launching pad is the rocket, taller than a thirty-story building. It is supported by a frame called a *gantry*.

At launching time you and the other spacemen ride in the elevator up the gantry, past the first two (or maybe three) stages, to the last stage, which is the nose of the rocket. You climb aboard and fasten the door behind you. After a final check of all the controls, you lie down on your chair beds, strap yourselves in, and wait.

The men in the rocket have nothing to do with sending it off into orbit. This job is so complicated that it is controlled and timed by the machines on the ground. In the control room there, the countdown has started. A buzzer rings in the cabin where you are waiting.

You cannot see the great flame at the base of the first

stage, but you hear the tremendous, screaming blast, and you are off to space.

For a few seconds the acceleration is so great that you feel as if you were being squashed, but you know the feeling won't last long. You start straight up. To the people watching from the ground the rocket seems to be going very slowly for a couple of seconds, almost standing on the exhaust flame. Then it goes faster and faster, and in 20 seconds it is out of sight, except to the trackers on the radar scope.

In a little more than a minute the bottom stage has used up all its fuel, and it drops away, into the sea. You are flattened against your couch again as the next stage fires and the rocket roars on up.

In another couple of minutes the fuel in the second stage is used up, and that drops off too. Now you have passed through the thickest part of the atmosphere. You are going faster every second. If there is another stage under the payload, that has dropped away too. The rocket motors of the last stage are burning, then they cut off and you are coasting. Less than five minutes after take-off you are out in space. Through the portholes you can see the earth, looking much larger than the moon ever looked.

Even though you are going thousands of miles an hour you don't have any feeling of motion. One reason you feel motion

on earth is that some of the things around you are standing still. It's the changing landscape as you speed by, or the bumps in the road, that tell you you're moving.

But did you ever sit in a train, alongside another train, both standing still in the station? The other train starts to move — or is it yours? For a few seconds you can't tell whether you are moving, standing still, or even going backwards.

In space, there is nothing outside your ship to show you whether you are moving, or how fast. For the same reason you don't feel yourself flying through space with the earth at more than 66,000 miles an hour.

63

Because the speed of the rocket in orbit exactly balances the pull of gravity, the ship has no weight and neither have you. When you unbuckle your safety belt you float around the cabin.

Zero gravity makes eating in space very different from eating on earth. You will have to drink out of a squeeze bottle. You cannot pour liquid as you do on earth, because it is gravity that makes it pour. You cannot eat out of a plate because your food would float off it. You might have to eat everything from a tube, somewhat as if you were squeezing toothpaste into your mouth. There cannot be anything to cut, because cutting would send things flying. There cannot be any bones or shells, because getting rid of garbage will be a problem.

You will even be able to eat the stuff your food is packaged in, just as you eat a vitamin pill, case and all. Maybe the case will taste like chocolate or marshmallow and you can eat it for dessert.

The air in the space ship is weightless too, and pumps will keep it moving. If they didn't, the stale air you breathed out would hang right in front of your nose and you wouldn't get any fresh air.

What will happen to that stale air, anyway? Probably the same thing that happens to it on earth. In the space ship there are many green plants, possibly algae, the simplest kind of green plants. Green plants take in carbon dioxide, the waste gas we breathe out, and they give off the oxygen we need.

Getting rid of wastes is a space problem. A space litterbug would find his litter orbiting right along with him. Soon he would be flying in a cloud of gum wrappers, banana peels, and dirty water frozen into ice crystals. Dirty wash water and stale air can be purified and used again, but things that can't be must be stored until they can be disposed of back on earth.

Now that you are coasting, you will want to step outside for a better look around. Of course, you can't just open the door and go. You have to put on your space suit. Inside, you've been wearing loose, comfortable clothes, but they will never do out in space. Your life depends on your space suit. Just as the cabin of the rocket is a small world with the atmosphere you need, your space suit is an even smaller one.

66

Your suit has to be strong to keep the pressure of the air inside from bursting it, but it has to be flexible enough so that you can move easily. It might be made of rubberized nylon, or some material that has not yet been invented. It will have a built-in air conditioner to keep you cool in the sun and to carry off the heat of your body, the stale air you breathe out, and the dampness you perspire.

Tanks on your back will supply the oxygen and air pressure you need.

The window in your helmet is specially made to shield your eyes from the sun's harmful rays.

Your space gloves probably won't have fingers. They might end in tools with inside controls that you can work with your fingers.

Your boots will have mag-

nets on the bottom so that you can stand or walk on the outside of the space ship without floating away. They will be insulated, too, so that you can walk on hot or cold space ships (or planets) without burning or freezing your feet.

You will have a safety rope, a radio in your helmet for talking to other spacemen, and an air jet for moving yourself around — just a little jet, like a bug bomb.

Now you are all equipped. You can go from the airtight compartment out into space.

In all directions the sky is black, even though the sun is shining brilliantly. There are no air particles to reflect the sun's light. The stars are shining too, like jewels of many colors. Now you know why astronomers want to get up above the atmosphere to look.

The side of the space ship facing the sun is very bright and hot. The side away from the sun is dark and very cold. You are half bright and half dark, half hot and half cold, too.

You tie yourself securely with your safety rope and drift away from the ship a little. There is no up and no down — only *out* from the space ship.

Now it's time to get down to work, for of course you've come to do a job. It will be a long time before anyone goes to space just to see the sights; there are too many things to do first.

Maybe you've come to build a space station that will be a base of operations in space. It will be an island where spacemen can observe, experiment, make charts, pick up supplies, and finally take off for other planets.

69

Things are very busy in the orbit. Other ships have brought more spacemen. Rocket trains have brought loads of building materials that float in the orbit where they have been dumped. The spacemen, the space ships, and the cargo are all satellites of the earth, whirling around it at a terrific speed even though you yourself don't feel that you are moving at all.

One squirt of your air jet sends you sailing wherever you are needed. (It's the third law of motion again; the air goes one way, you go the other.) Because nothing has weight, you can push huge pieces of metal around easily. Some spacemen are working in one-man, low-powered rockets. Others are hammering and riveting, but there isn't a sound.

Sound travels through something, not through empty space.

The foreman gives directions by radio. The only time you can hear another spaceman without the radio is when you are both touching the same thing or each other. Sound travels very well through solid things, and because it does you can hear him.

When it's lunchtime, you have to go back inside the ship. You can't simply sit down and have a sandwich the way a worker does on earth. It would be more dangerous for a spaceman to open his helmet in space than it would be for a diver deep under the sea to open his.

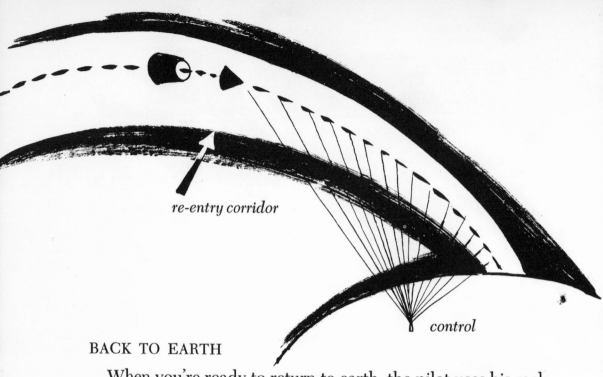

re-entry corridor

control

BACK TO EARTH

When you're ready to return to earth, the pilot uses his rockets to steer the space ship into the *re-entry corridor*, which is like an entrance hall back to earth. You'd better be strapped into your couch when those rockets go on again, because suddenly you are no longer weightless. The pressure of acceleration or of slowing down makes you very, very heavy.

Once you are in the re-entry corridor, the tracking stations and the control center start correcting the position of the ship, and guiding it in.

Here you might drop a last part of your spacecraft — the stage that carries your rocket engines and all the equipment you have been using in space. It will stay in orbit until a service ship picks it up. Now only the crew's quarters at the very front are left for the control center to bring back to earth.

72

As you hurtle back through the atmosphere, the pressure is enormous — the greatest you have had. The heat on the capsule is enormous, too, and makes it glow and flame like a hot coal.

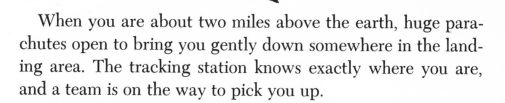

When you are about two miles above the earth, huge parachutes open to bring you gently down somewhere in the landing area. The tracking station knows exactly where you are, and a team is on the way to pick you up.

But before long, if you're a real spaceman, you'll be on your way again, out to the space station or maybe even farther into space.

73

SPACE STATIONS AND SPACE SHIPS

The space station might be shaped like a ball, or a saucer, or a wheel. It might be two balls connected by a rod. But it will certainly be turning. Here's the reason.

Most scientists agree that for short trips, even trips of several weeks, weightlessness probably won't bother anybody. They don't know how you would feel if you were weightless for a long time, however. Because you wouldn't need to use your muscles, they might stop working. You might lose your sense of balance. Your heart is a kind of gravity pump, and it might not work right after a while.

The space station will be built so that it *seems* to have gravity. It will use a force called *centrifugal force*.

Did you ever put a small object on a spinning phonograph record and watch it move off toward the rim? Did you ever ride a revolving platform at an amusement park, and feel yourself pulled toward the edge? Centrifugal force was working.

Centrifugal force pulls you out toward the edge

If a space station shaped like a wheel was turning, everything in it would be pulled toward the outer rim, in the same way gravity pulls you toward the earth. The outer rim would be "down," and the center of the space station would be "up." The closer you got to the center, the less weight you would have.

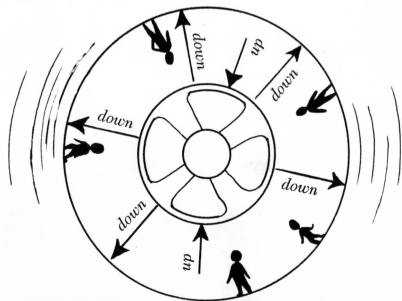

A space station might be built like this.

Taxi port

Meteor bumper

Many kinds of scientists work in the space station. They study the stars and the weather, make maps of the earth, and charts of the sky. There are botanists, biologists, chemists, doctors, and engineers. There are mechanics, navigators, photographers, and repairmen.

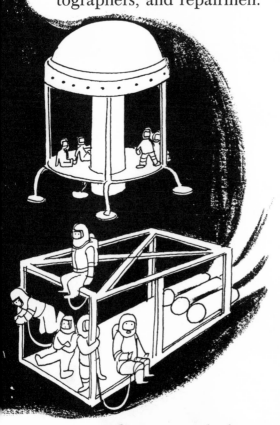

The space station is also a supply depot, and a place for building other kinds of space ships. Because these can take off from the space station, they do not need the thrust of the earth-to-orbit rockets. Because there is no atmosphere to cut through, they don't have to be streamlined. Because they don't have to stand the terrible pressures of take-off and landing on earth, they can be built lightly. These space ships will be exploring ships, observation platforms, space taxis, and supply ferries, each designed to do its own kind of job.

Someday space platforms will be real cities in space, with whole families living on them, growing their own food, working at their jobs, keeping house, watching television, and going to school.

WHERE TO?

When you take off from the space station, where are you going out in space?

We have a pretty good idea where you're *not* going. You're not going to the sun. It is so hot — thousands of degrees at the surface, millions of degrees inside — that you'd burn to a crisp long before you got there. Besides, it is so heavy and has such tremendous gravity that if you got within millions of miles of it you would never get away. The sun's gravity is so strong that it holds the planet Pluto in orbit, 3,700 million miles away.

You won't travel among the other stars, either. They are too far away.

THE MOON

The moon will surely be your first stop in exploring space. We know a lot of things about the moon. We even

have maps of the mountains and craters on the side that faces the earth, and some pictures of the other side. As space goes, it is very near — only about 238,000 miles away. The trip will be short. The moon's gravity is only one-sixth as strong as the earth's, so you won't have much trouble taking off again. But the moon's gravity isn't even strong enough to hold an atmosphere, so you'll have to wear your space suit all the time. (Unless, before you get there, an air-conditioned moon colony has been built under a plastic dome.)

Because there is no atmosphere, there is no weather on the moon — no wind or rain or snow. Meteors fall all the time, however — so many of them that the surface is covered with rocks and rock dust. Nothing grows there. Because there is no atmosphere to shield you from the sun, or to hold warmth when the sun isn't shining, the days are very hot and the nights are very cold.

The very bright "star" you sometimes see at sunset or sunrise is not a star at all, but the planet Venus

VENUS

You'll certainly want to explore Venus, our nearest planet. Sometimes it is only 24 million miles away. Venus is almost the same size as the earth. It is hotter, though, because it is closer to the sun.

Venus is a planet of mystery because it is surrounded by very thick clouds. We have never seen its surface. Our instruments have discovered water vapor in its atmosphere, so there must be some oxygen too. We don't know whether the light from the sun ever gets through the clouds, or whether the planet is always dark. To us, though, it looks very bright. We call it the morning or evening "star."

If there are intelligent creatures on Venus, they may not even know that the rest of the universe is there. The clouds that hide the planet from us probably hide the heavens from them.

MARS

When we talk about space travel we think about the planet Mars. Mars is about one-half the size of the earth. We know it has an atmosphere because we can see clouds there, but that atmosphere is much thinner than ours. Mars is quite cold, but it would be bearable to a person in a space suit. There may be a little water because we have seen frost or ice.

Are there any kinds of life? We don't know. Mars is crossed by a network of lines that some people used to think were canals. But no one has seen them close enough to find out what they really are — yet.

Mars has two very small moons called Phobos and Deimos. They are quite close to their planet, and they revolve around it much faster than any other moons in the solar system.

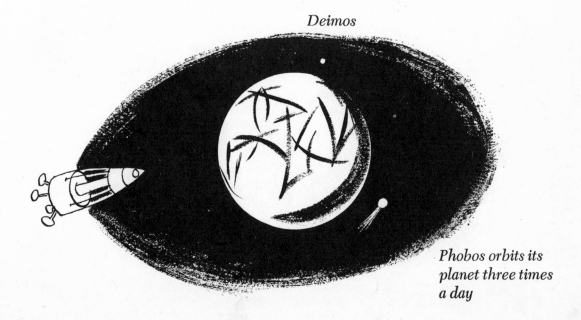

Deimos

*Phobos orbits its
planet three times
a day*

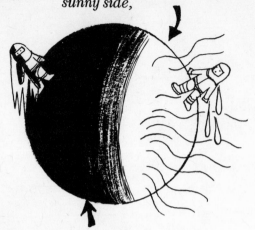

You would melt on the sunny side,

and freeze on the dark side,

but you might be comfortable in between

MERCURY

One planet you won't want to visit is Mercury. It is so near the sun that the side facing the sun is hot enough to melt lead. The always-dark side is so cold that air would freeze. Where the dark and the bright sides meet, however, the climate might be something like that of the moon. It seems to have little or no atmosphere, and is a barren rock.

THE ASTEROIDS

Between Mars and Jupiter is a great stretch of space where thousands of tiny satellites orbit. Some are no larger than little houses, but some are several hundred miles across. It would be interesting to land on the bigger ones, even though there wouldn't be much to see but rock.

Between Mars and Jupiter are the asteroids

THE COLD PLANETS

The first two planets be-
yond the asteroids are the
giants Jupiter and Saturn.
Both are more than ten times
larger than the earth. Both are
so cold that their atmospheres
are frozen into a sort of icy
slush. These atmospheres
aren't like ours, however. They
are mostly marsh gas and am-
monia — poison to us.

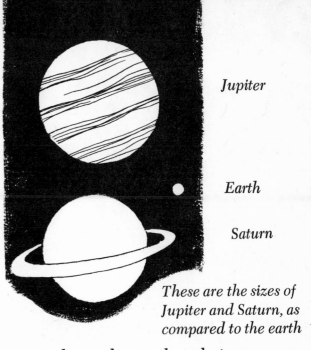

Jupiter

Earth

Saturn

*These are the sizes of
Jupiter and Saturn, as
compared to the earth*

You wouldn't want to get too near these planets, but their
moons will be good for exploring, and there are plenty of
those. Jupiter has twelve moons, and Saturn has nine. You
will also want to get a good look at Saturn's famous rings.
These are probably what is left of another moon that broke
into billions of tiny bits which still whirl around the planet.

URANUS, NEPTUNE, AND PLUTO

The outer planets are so far
away that they are even cold-
er than Jupiter and Saturn.
If you were standing on Pluto,
the farthest, the sun would
look like a very bright star.

83

ANYBODY UP THERE?

Are there intelligent beings on other planets in our solar system? Most scientists don't think so. If there are, the only likely places are Venus and Mars.

It is fun to imagine our kind of humans on other worlds, but they would probably look so different we might not recognize them as people at all. Living things have a wonderful way of adapting themselves to conditions around them in order to stay alive. Plants grow in the Arctic. Some simple animals can survive being boiled or frozen. Creatures live in the blackest deeps of the sea under thousands of tons of pressure.

We can't really say that our kind of air is the only kind living things could breathe, or that they must have water or a certain climate. Creatures that breathed other gases or lived in temperatures that would kill earthmen, however, certainly wouldn't look like us.

84

Are there people anywhere else in the universe? Maybe there are. One radio telescope explores space for intelligent signals. If they come, scientists think they will be in the form of a mathematical formula.

In our own galaxy there are billions of stars. Some must have planets with conditions like those on earth. Somewhere in space there could be other thinking beings. If their planets are older, they may know more than we do. They may be already traveling in space.

85

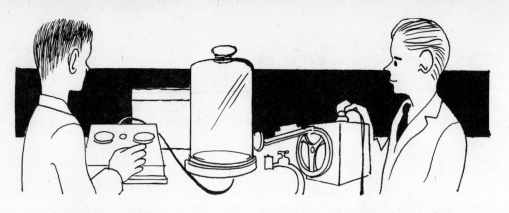

SCIENTISTS ARE WORKING ON THESE THINGS, AND MORE

1. NEW KINDS OF POWER FOR ROCKETS AND SATELLITES

The problem is to get more power from less fuel. A nuclear rocket would be the answer. A small amount of fuel, heated in an atomic engine, called a reactor, could be changed into a great amount of thrust. But a reactor gets hot enough to melt the walls of the rocket. Scientists are working on the idea of holding this hot fuel in an invisible bottle made of magnetic force.

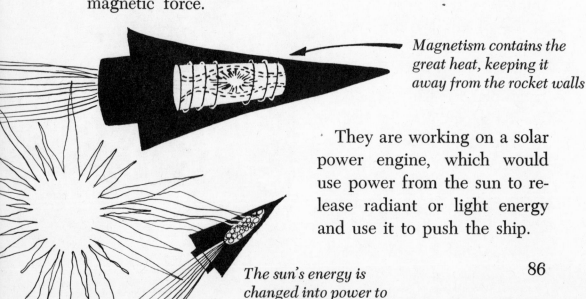

Magnetism contains the great heat, keeping it away from the rocket walls

They are working on a solar power engine, which would use power from the sun to release radiant or light energy and use it to push the ship.

The sun's energy is changed into power to run the ship

They are experimenting with using electricity to send a powerful charge into the propellant, then speeding it up with magnets and shooting it out fast through a kind of electron gun something like the one in a television tube.

2. AIRPLANES INTO SPACE

Spacecraft in the lower levels of space must be controlled from the ground. They must be put up from special launching places and brought down into special recovery areas. Engineers are developing airplanes that a pilot can operate in lower space, and that he can land anywhere.

3. FOOD IN SPACE

Growing and keeping food will be a problem. Botanists are working to develop plants that will grow fast, without soil, at low or zero gravity, and that will taste good and not be harmed by cosmic rays. Without gravity, do you think roots will grow down and stems grow up?

Because cans and freezers are not practical in space, experts are finding new ways to preserve food — by irradiation, shooting the food full of a kind of electric charge, and by freeze-drying, which removes 90 per cent of its weight.

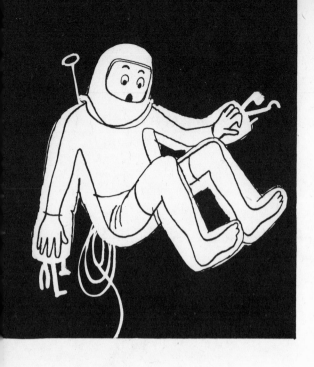

4. NEW KINDS OF MATERIALS

We do not know what will happen to the metals, machinery, lubricants, and paints we use on earth when they have been in zero gravity over a length of time, or in a total vacuum, a place completely without air. We may have to develop new kinds of materials for use in space.

SLEEP YOUR WAY TO SPACE

Some trips through space will take a long, long time. Scientists are experimenting with "frozen sleep," which is almost a kind of hibernation, similar to that of some animals that sleep through the winter. By the time the hibernating space travelers wake up, they will be close to their destination.

WE DON'T KNOW MUCH ABOUT

1. COSMIC RAYS

The very powerful waves of energy from the sun and stars can penetrate any known material. They are more abundant in space than in the atmosphere and they can go through the walls of a rocket just as light goes through a window. We cannot feel them, but are they harmful? What will happen to men in space who are exposed to these rays for a length of time? Nobody knows yet.

2. SPACE AND TIME

Part of Einstein's theory of relativity says that when anything goes very, very fast, approaching the speed of light, time slows down for that thing. If this is true and we can reach these speeds, it will make a great difference in the time it takes to travel through space. Someday we'll find out about that.

TOMORROW IN SPACE

Nobody knows how soon man will be standing on the other planets, or how far in space he can go. Not many years ago space travel was a science fiction idea. But, not too long before that, so were flying, and talking and seeing across space, and harnessing atoms, and building machines to think and figure for us.

Nobody knows what discoveries will be made tomorrow or next week or next year, or what inventions will grow out of these discoveries. But some of them will surely take us into worlds that are still unexplored, either here on earth or out among the stars.

INDEX

FIRST BOOKS
Complete Check List

Series No.	Quantity	TITLE	Author	A	sl	L	C	CS	H	Grade Reading Level
68		Atlas	C S Hammond & Co	A	sl	L				3-4
22		Africa	Hughes	A	sl	L		CS		4-7
140		Air	Knight	A	sl	L				4 up
1		Airplanes	Bendick	A	sl	L	C	CS		3-6
76		American History	Commager	A	sl	L	C	CS		4 up
11		The American Revolution	Morris	A	sl	L	C	CS		5 up
158		Ancient Bible Lands	Robinson							New Publication
134		Ancient Egypt	Robinson	A		L				4 up
110		Ancient Greece	Robinson	A		L				4 up
150		Ancient Mesopotamia and Persia	Robinson	A		L				4 up
99		Ancient Rome	Robinson	A		L				4 up
73		The Antarctic	Icenhower	A		L	C			4-7
77		Archaeology	Kubie	A	sl	L	C	CS		4 up
135		Architecture	Moore	A	sl	L				4 up
104		Astronomy	Grey	A		L				4 up
107		Australia	Kaula			L				4-7
5		Automobiles	Bendick	A	sl	L	C	CS		3-5
44		The Ballet	Streatfeild	A	sl	L		CS		4-7
148		Barbarian Invaders	Sobol	A						5 up
14		Baseball	Brewster	A	sl	L	C	CS		3-5
94		Basketball	Schiffer	A	sl	L	C			4-8
4		Bees	Tibbets			L	C	CS		3-6
98		Bells	Fletcher					CS		2-4
18		Birds	Williamson	A	sl	L	C	CS		3-6
2		Boats	Gossett	A		L		CS		2-4
101		Boys' Cooking	Beim	A	sl	L	C	CS		4 up
149		Brazil	Sheppard	A						4 up
43		Bridges	Peet	A		L	C	CS		3-7
6		Bugs	Williamson	A	sl	L	C	CS	H	3-5
153		California Gold Rush	Havighurst	A		L				4-7
65		Canada	C & M Lineaweaver	A		L	C			4-6
139		Cartoons for Kids	Fenner							2-5
111		Cats	Taber	A	sl	L	C			3-6
54		Caves	E Hamilton	A	sl	L	C			4-6
45		Chess	Leeming	A	sl	L	C	CS	H	5 up
173		The China Clippers	Rich							New Publication
146		Christmas Joy	Wilson	A		L				1-3
105		Civil War Land Battles	Dupuy	A	sl	L	C			5 up
137		Civil War Naval Actions	Dupuy	A	sl	L				5 up
29		Codes and Ciphers	S & B Epstein	A	sl	L	C	CS	H	3-5
95		Color	Paschel	A		L	C	CS		5 up
157		Comunist China	Kinmond							New Publication
108		The Congo	McDonnell			L				3-6
9		Congress	Coy	A	sl	L	C		H	5 up
47		Conservation	F C Smith	A	sl	L	C	CS		4-7
85		The Constitution	Morris	A	sl	L	C	CS		5 up
40		Cotton	Rogers	A		L	C	CS		4-6
13		Cowboys	Brewster	A	sl	L	C	CS		4 up
10		Dogs	Taber	A		L	C	CS		3-5
39		Dolls	H Hoke	A	sl	L	C	CS		1-3
88		Drawing	Slobodkin	A	sl	L	C			6 up
96		The Early Settlers	Rich	A	sl	L	C			4-6
81		The Earth	Sevrey	A		L	C			5 up
42		Electricity	S & B Epstein	A	sl	L	C	CS		4-8
83		England	Streatfeild	A		L	C	CS		4-7
26		Eskimos	Brewster	A	sl	L	C	CS		3-5
79		Fairy Tales	Abell							3 up
25		Festivals	Reck	A		L	C			3-6
21		Firemen	Brewster	A		L				3-5
69		Food	Scheib	A		L	C	CS		3-5
87		Football	Schiffer	A	sl	L	C			3 u
92		France	Gottlieb	A	sl	L	C			4-7
61		Gardening	Kirkus	A	sl	L	C			4-6
122		Ghana	Lobsenz	A	sl	L				4-7
155		Glaciers	Marcus	A		L				4 u
60		Glass	S & B Epstein	A		L	C	CS		3-5
48		Hawaii	S & B Epstein	A		L	C	CS		4-6
62		Holidays	Burnett	A		L	C			3-5
8		Horses	McMeekin	A	sl	L	C	CS		5 u
129		How to Fix It	Bendick-Berk	A	sl	L				3 u
143		Human Senses	Liberty	A	sl	L				4 u
66		India	Hahn			L	C	CS		4-7
103		The Indian Wars	Morris	A						4 u
15		Indians (American)	Brewster	A		L	C	CS		2-6
41		Israel	Kubie	A	sl	L				4-7
89		Italy	S & B Epstein	A		L	C	CS		4-7
30		Japan	Mears	A		L	C	CS		4-7
58		Jazz	Hughes	A		L	C	CS	H	7 u
19		Jokes	Chrystie	A		L	C	CS		3-6
130		Kings	Newton			L				3-6
172		Language & How To Use It	Applegate							New Publication
159		Legendary Beings	Jacobson							New Publication
74		Letter Writing	Jacobson	A		L	C	CS		4-6
160		Light	Harrison							New Publication
152		Machines	Buehr	A						3-6
46		Magic	Stoddard	A	sl	L	C			3-5
75		Mammals	Williamson	A	sl	L	C	CS	H	4 u
90		Maps and Globes	S & B Epstein	A	sl	L	C	CS		4-6
125		Measurement	S & B Epstein			L				4-6
102		Medieval Man	Sobol	A	sl	L				4 u
123		The Mediterranean	Gottlieb	A		L				4-7
63		Mexico	S & B Epstein	A		L	C		H	4-7
35		Microbes	Lewis	A	sl	L	C	CS	H	4 u
116		Mining	Markun	A		L				3-6
51		Music	Norman	A	sl	L	C			3-6
128		Mythical Beasts	Jacobson	A		L				3-5
67		Mythology	Elgin	A		L		CS		4 u
113		National Monuments	Lobsenz	A		L				3 u
115		National Parks	Lobsenz	A		L				3 u
27		Negroes	Hughes	A	sl	L	C	CS		4 u
154		Netherlands	Cohn	A						4 u
12		New England	Rich	A				CS	H	4-6
119		New World Explorers	Rich	A		L				4-6
131		New Zealand	Kaula	A						4 u
72		Norse Legends	Elgin			L				4-6
16		Nurses	Elting	A	sl	L	C			3-5
133		Ocean	Epstein	A		L				4 u
109		The Oregon Trail	Havighurst	A		L	C			3-7
118		Paintings	Moore	A		L	C			4 u
151		Pakistan	Bothwell	A		L				4 u
84		The Panama Canal	Markun	A	sl	L	C	CS		4 u
50		Photography	J Hoke	A	sl	L	C	CS	H	5 u
142		Physical Fitness	Walsh	A		L				4 u
97		Pioneers	Havighurst							4-8
38		Plants	Dickinson	A			C	CS		4 u
37		Poetry	Peterson	A	sl	L	C	CS		3-6
53		Prehistoric Animals	Dickinson	A	sl	L	C	CS		4-7
28		Presidents	Coy	A		L		CS		4 u
64		Printing	S & B Epstein	A	sl	L	C	CS	H	5 u
114		Public Libraries	Graham			L				2-4
24		Puppets	Jagendorf	A		L	C			3-5
49		Rhythms	Hughes	A	sl	L	C	CS		2-4
55		Roads	Bothwell	A	sl	L	C	CS		4-6
136		Sailing	M Lineaweaver	A		L	C	CS		8 u
31		Science Experiments	Wyler	A	sl	L	C			4-6

ALL are supplied in the Watts Guaranteed Library Binding

ALL are in large, clear type

ALL are fully illustrated—many with over 100 pictures, and in color

ALL checked and double-checked for accuracy, authority, and clarity of text

ALL 7¼ x 8¾ size

KEY TO LISTINGS:

A   American Library Association, Booklist
sl   Booklist, Small Library Listing
L   Library Journal
C   H. W. Wilson Company, Children's Catalog
CS   Child Study Association of America, Books of the Year for Children
H   H. W. Wilson Company, High School Catalog

What they say about FIRST BOOKS

"Their wide appeal, their broad coverage of varied subject areas, their wide range of significant and timely topics, and their attractive format and illustrations have made them valuable library materials."

MIRIAM PETERSON
Chicago Board of Education

"The format of each book has been superior and the books show that careful attention has been given to design, type, illustration, paper, and binding."

CAROLYN W. FIELD
Philadelphia Public Library

"I have long felt that the FIRST BOOKS developed (by Franklin Watts) were among the important creative contributions made by a publisher in recent decades."

PROF. HAROLD G. SHANE
Indiana University

"I really don't know how we ever ran our school libraries without the FIRST BOOKS!"

ELIZABETH HODGES
Baltimore Board of Education

"In covering a topic thoroughly, these books are like a junior encyclopedia, with an illustrated volume for each subject."

Christian Science Monitor

"Indeed an achievement! The high quality which has been maintained throughout the series is even more remarkable."

RUTH HILL VIGUERS
The Horn Book

"The FIRST BOOKS have made a real contribution in extending the horizons of their readers beyond the interests they knew they had."

JOSETTE FRANK
Child Study Association of America

Write for catalog. Address Dept. Sc

FRANKLIN WATTS, INC. A Division

575 Lexington Avenue   **New York 22, N. Y.**   of Grolier Incorporated

629.4
B
BENDICK, JEANNE
    First book of space travel